Real-World Math

Grades 3–4

Strengthen the Math Skills
Needed in Everyday Life

by Susan Carroll

Carson-Dellosa Publishing Company, Inc.
Greensboro, North Carolina

Credits

Editor
Susan Morris

Layout Design
Jon Nawrocik

Artists
Van Harris
Jon Nawrocik

Cover Design
Annette Hollister-Papp

Cover and Inside Photos
Photo www.comstock.com
© 1993 Digital Wisdom, Inc.
© 2001 Brand X Pictures
© 1999 EyeWire, Inc. All rights reserved.
© 1998 Digital Stock Corporation.
© Photodisc
© Corbis Images
© Dynamic Graphics, Inc.

ISBN 1-59441-053-4

Table of Contents

About This Book...

Math is everywhere!

Real-World Math was written to connect mathematics to real-world problems that students encounter in their daily lives. The activities in this book are designed to help students become independent problem solvers as they use patterns, elapsed time, calendars, measurement, money, and other mathematical concepts to solve problems.

The book contains 14 activities that focus on real-world problems. While using the picture at the beginning of each activity as a reference, students can demonstrate problem-solving skills by answering the questions on the following pages. Copies of each picture should be provided for the students. Each picture is followed by two activity pages with short-answer and multiple-choice questions. The first activity page is geared toward lower-level thinking skills while the second activity page progresses through higher-level thinking. The two different formats allows you to differentiate how to use the activity for the varying learning levels of students.

A teacher notes and extensions section follows each activity. Each section includes a description of the picture that students will use to complete the worksheets. Review this description with students prior to having them complete the worksheets. The teacher notes contain teaching strategies and ideas for instruction. For example, Grocery Shopping (page 20) has suggestions for teaching converting decimals to fractions and percents. Planning a Garden (page 28) suggests an oral and kinesthetic approach to learning the names of different kinds of angles. The teacher notes are designed to use as needed. In addition, theme-based extension activities are included. These activities are intended to give other options for expanding students' knowledge on the subject or providing cross-curricular connections. For example, Checks and Balances (page 12) suggest that students discuss the types of bills their families pay each month. Students can compare and contrast the kinds of bills their families pay and graph the information. Using these ideas allows you to extend students' knowledge, as well as vary the activities according to students' needs.

As students use the activities in this book, they will begin to make more mathematical connections to the world in which they live. They will see that math truly is everywhere.

Array of Hope

Looking for My Data	5:52
Does This Mean It's Average?	4:30
Taking a Chance	3:25
I Can Count on You	3:52
Let's Be Rational	4:07
Total Ellipse, Not the Heart	2:59
Every Little Thing She Does Is Math	3:11
Tessellations Rhapsody	4:05

groove tactics

Get to the Vertex

Sign of the Times	5:10
Gee, I'm a Tree	3:37
Sum Thing to Add About	4:21
You Just Let Time Elapse	3:15
What Do We Have in Common?	3:56
I've Noticed a Pattern	3:00
Mustang Tally	4:06

sick records   NOTHING'S IMPOSSIBLE

Think Outside the Cube

You're My Sweetie Pi	5:01
My Octopus Went Octagon	4:13
Just a Segment	3:41
Come on Scalene	2:50
We Are Fact Families	3:05
Prime After Prime	4:17
Susie Cubed	3:26

Mixing Music

Use the CD covers to answer the questions.

1. Abby and Felicia are looking for a song to dance to at the talent show. They have $4\frac{1}{2}$ minutes for their dance. Which song on *Get to the Vertex* is about $4\frac{1}{2}$ minutes long?

2. The stage crew needs music to play while they set up the stage for the next talent show act. If they have 3-4 minutes between acts, how many song choices do they have on the 3 CDs?

3. Devon listened to all of the songs on *Array of Hope* on the school bus. About how long was his ride on the school bus?

4. Bart fell asleep while listening to music. He remembers hearing the beginning of "Taking a Chance." His mother woke him up at the end of "Total Ellipse, Not the Heart." About how long was he asleep?
   a. 11 minutes   c. 14 minutes
   b. 7 minutes   d. 18 minutes

5. Jay started listening to *Think Outside the Cube* at 4:00 P.M. What time was it when he finished listening to the CD?

6. What is the total length of the *Get to the Vertex* CD?

7. Fabio wants a CD to listen to while he goes running. If he runs for 30 minutes, which CD should he listen to if he wants to listen to music the entire time?

8. Mario noticed a big difference between the song lengths on his CD. Which song on *Array of Hope* is about $\frac{1}{2}$ the length of "Looking for My Data"?

9. Caroline thinks she is getting more music for her money when she gets more minutes on a CD. If all CDs are the same price, which CD does Caroline think is the best deal?

10. Xander wanted to make 1 CD from the 3 CDs he bought to listen to during his drive to work. If he used the 2 longest songs from each CD, how long was the CD that Xander made?
    a. 27 minutes 13 seconds
    b. 29 minutes 11 seconds
    c. 24 minutes 38 seconds
    d. 31 minutes 22 seconds

Mixing Music

Use the CD covers to answer the questions.

Put the CDs in order from longest running time to shortest. Write the names and total running times of the CDs on the lines.

1. _____

2. _____

3. _____

4. If the songs on *Think Outside the Cube* were played in order from longest to shortest, which song would be played in the middle?

5. Billy listened to all of the songs on *Get to the Vertex* and the first half of the songs on *Array of Hope* before he got to his grandmother's house. About how long was the drive?

6. Tessa was asked to describe the length of the songs on *Think Outside the Cube*. What is the difference between the longest song and the shortest song?

7. Trisha's favorite song is "Sum Thing to Add About." Her least favorite song on the same CD is 44 seconds shorter. What is her least favorite song?

8. Monika wanted to have her room cleaned in the time it took her to listen to all 3 CDs. How long does Monika want to spend cleaning her room? (Round to the nearest half hour.)
   a. $\frac{1}{2}$ hour   c. $1\frac{1}{2}$ hours
   b. 1 hour   d. 2 hours

9. The woman at the CD store told Jeremy that the average song on *Array of Hope* is about 4 minutes long. Was the woman at the CD store correct?

10. Which CD has half the songs that are less than 4 minutes in length?

11. What percentage of songs on *Array of Hope* are shorter than "Does This Mean It's Average"?

12. Gabe wanted to do a karate routine to "Prime After Prime." However, the song was 10 seconds too long. Which song is the same length as his routine?

13. Alberto wanted to make his own greatest hits CD from the 3 CDs he bought. He wants the CD to have 30 minutes of music. What is the greatest number of songs he can fit on the CD?
   a. 7   c. 9
   b. 8   d. 10

Mixing Music

The Picture:

The picture is three music CDs. Each CD lists song titles and song lengths. On CDs, song lengths are listed in minutes and seconds separated by colons.

Teacher Notes:

Model for students how to add minutes and seconds using the following method:

1. List the minutes in one column and the seconds in another column.
2. Add the numbers in the seconds column.
3. If the total is greater than 60, subtract 60 from the total and add 1 to the minutes column.
4. Repeat step 3 until you can no longer subtract 60. The remainder will be the total number of seconds.
5. Add the minutes to the seconds that were carried over to get the total number of minutes.

Explain that each song on a CD is a fractional part of the total number of songs on the CD. The total number of songs on the CD is the denominator. The numerator would be individual songs.

Extension Activities:

1. Let students listen to pre-approved music CDs and time the songs using the second hand on a clock. Then, have students determine the total amount of music recorded on the CD.
2. In conjunction with the music department at your school, create a CD of students' singing. Let students design the CD cover. (This works especially well for holidays.) Sell copies of the CD as a fund-raiser for the school.
3. Have students compare the length of classical instrumentals to modern lyrical songs. Choose two songs that are the same length. Let students listen to each song, then predict if one song is longer, shorter, or the same as the other. Have students check their predictions by playing the songs again and using a second hand or stopwatch to test their predictions.
4. Let the class determine if tempo affects speed. Tell students that they will jump rope while listening to music. Have students predict how many times they can jump rope during a one-minute excerpt of music. Begin with a song that has a fast tempo. Have them count the number of jumps they can complete. Let them repeat the activity with a song that has a slower tempo. Explain that even though students are not told to jump to the tempo of the music, they are more inclined to do so. Let them compare their results to their predictions.

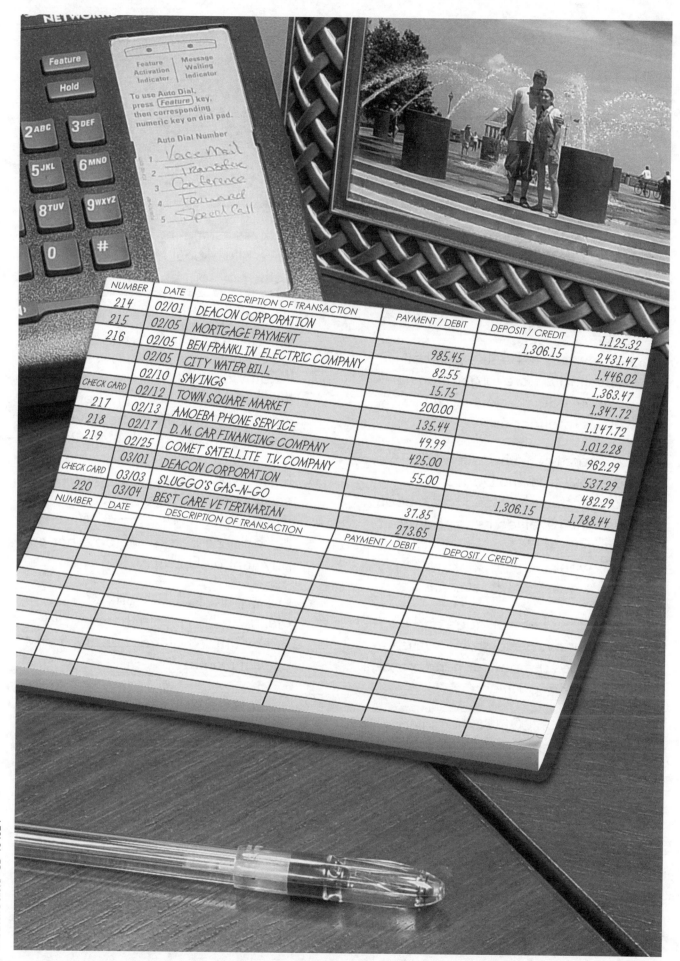

Name _____

Checks and Balances

Use the checkbook to answer the questions.

1. When looking at her checkbook, Kathy noticed that she had more payments than credits. How many total payments did Kathy record in her checkbook?

2. Kathy wants to be sure that her deposit totals are larger than her payments/debits. How much are Kathy's total deposits?

3. On March 1, Kathy received a deposit from the Deacon Corporation. How long had it been since she received her last deposit from it?
   a. 1 week   c. 25 days
   b. 3 weeks   d. 1 month

4. Kathy pays her mortgage and car payment every month. How much more does she pay for her mortgage than her car payment?

5. Kathy puts $200.00 in her savings account every month in case of emergencies. On March 3, she had an unexpected veterinarian bill. How much more did Kathy pay for the veterinarian than she put in her savings in March?

6. Kathy is estimating the amount of some bills. About how much did Kathy pay for her phone, satellite TV, and water bills?
   a. $100.00   c. $120.00
   b. $115.00   d. $125.00

7. If Kathy deposits the same amount into her savings account every month, how much will she have saved at the end of the year?

8. Kathy wants to be sure that she has enough money in her account before she pays her car payment. What is her balance before she pays her car payment on February 17?

9. Kathy paid $23.19 more for electricity this month than she did last month. What was her electricity bill last month?

10. Kathy went to the bank and gave the teller some $10.00 bills to be put into her savings account. How many $10.00 bills did she give the teller?

11. What fraction of 1 dollar is the change on Kathy's water bill payment?

CD-104024 • Real-World Math

Checks and Balances

Use the checkbook to answer the questions.

1. What is the total of Kathy's deposits on the current checkbook register?

2. After adding the deposit to the previous page's total, Kathy began subtracting her payments. What was the date her balance was $1,147.72?
   a. February 5   c. February 17
   b. February 10   d. February 25

3. Kathy's husband asked her to write checks for the 2 bills whose total is $480.00. Which 2 bills did Kathy pay?

4. The last time that Kathy was paid by the Deacon Corporation was March 1. On what date will she be paid next?

5. One of Kathy's receipts has an itemized list of $110.00, $10.20, and $15.24. Which transaction was this?

6. When Kathy wrote out the amount of the check for the electric bill, she wrote the amount of change as a fraction. What would the amount of change look like as a fraction?

7. If Kathy keeps track of all deposits and withdrawals in her checkbook register, how much money was in her account on February 21?

8. What percentage of Kathy's monthly deposit from the Deacon Corporation goes toward her mortgage payment?

9. After Kathy balanced her checkbook through March 4, what was her ending balance?

10. On March 5, Kathy must pay an insurance bill that is $1,500.00. Does she have enough money to pay the bill?

11. In April, Kathy received a 10% salary raise from the Deacon Corporation. How much is her new monthly salary?

12. Kathy was excited about the raise in salary that she received. She decided to save the additional money for a vacation in December. How much money will she have saved at the end of the year?

Checks and Balances

The Picture:

The picture is a checkbook register. There are two deposits and 10 debits. The dates of the transactions are between February 1 and March 4. The balance from the previous page is recorded at the top of the right column.

Teacher Notes:

Teaching checkbook skills not only reinforces addition and subtraction skills, it also teaches students about home economics.

Show students how to record information in a checkbook register by explaining what information goes in each column.

- Column 1: Each check is numbered. Check numbers are recorded in the first column to keep track of checks that have been written.
- Column 2: The date column shows the dates on which the transactions take place.
- Column 3: The description of transaction column allows a person to briefly describe who is being paid with money from the account and who has contributed money to the account in the form of a deposit or credit.
- Column 4: The payment/debit column shows the amount of money going out of the checking account.
- Column 5: The deposit/credit column shows the amount of money coming into the checking account.
- Column 6: The balance from the previous page is carried over on the top row of this column. The following rows are for calculating the new balance after each transaction.

Extension Activities:

1. Have students ask their parents or guardians about some of the payments they make each month. Have each student bring in a list of five types of payments his parents or guardians make. Help students compare the lists by making a tally chart, then graphing the information.
2. Create a home budget for students to keep for a week. Assign groups of students different salaries, including minimum wage. Each day, have students add or subtract transactions that you have prepared, such as rent/mortgage, utility bills, gas, food, etc. (Use current prices for gas and groceries.) At the end of the week, let groups compare their ending balances.
3. For homework, have students help their parents or guardians balance their checkbooks one month.

February

Sunday	Monday	Tuesday	Wednesday	Thursday	Friday	Saturday
Celebrate Black History Month		1	2 Groundhog Day	3	4	5
6	7	8	9	10	11	12
13	14 Valentine's Day	15	16	17	18	19
20	21 Presidents' Day	22	23	24	25	26
27	28					

Calendar Challenge

Use the calendar to answer the questions.

1. How many days are between Valentine's Day and March 1?

2. Casper had chicken pox between Groundhog Day and Valentine's Day. How long was he sick?

3. Bill's birthday was 5 days before Presidents' Day. What is the date of Bill's birthday?

4. Timmy and Tommy split their paper route. Timmy delivers the papers on even dates. How many days in February does Tommy deliver the paper?

5. Jeannine and her 2 children went skiing every Saturday that it snowed in February. If they skied 3 times, what fraction of Saturdays did it snow?

    a. $\frac{1}{3}$ c. $\frac{3}{3}$

    b. $\frac{2}{3}$ d. $\frac{3}{4}$

6. Jacob has a Black History report due on February 25. If the report was assigned on February 4, how many days does he have to complete the report?

7. Michael has a scouts meeting every other Monday. If his last meeting was February 7, what is the date of his next meeting?

8. Susan passes out party invitations on February 8. The date of the party is 2 weeks and 2 days later. What is the date of her party?

9. Kali has ballet lessons every 3 days. If her first lesson was on February 15, how many more lessons will she have in February?

    a. 2   c. 4

    b. 3   d. 5

10. Marley began making her valentine cards on February 1. She made 2 cards each day. If she finished the last 2 cards February 13, how many cards did she make?

11. Jon goes to hockey practice every Tuesday and Thursday. How many times will he have practice in the month of February?

12. If Andrew reads 5 books every week in February, how many books will he have read by the end of the month?

Name _____

Calendar Challenge

Use the calendar to answer the questions.

1. José is writing his appointments on the calendar. He has a dentist appointment 2 weeks and 4 days before Presidents' Day. What is the date of José's appointment?

2. Ryan's grandmother is visiting on the second Saturday of the month. She is leaving on the third Wednesday. How long will she be visiting?

3. Stephanie takes swimming lessons every Thursday. What fraction of the month does she spend taking swimming lessons?
   a. $\frac{3}{28}$ c. $\frac{1}{4}$
   b. $\frac{1}{7}$ d. $\frac{1}{2}$

4. Devante washes cars each Saturday to earn money. He earns $5.00 per car. If he washed 3 cars each weekend, how much money did he earn in February?

5. The time the sun rises decreases about 1 minute daily between December and June. If the sun rises at 6:41 A.M. on February 2, what time will the sun rise on the last day in February?

6. The temperature on February 7 was 58°F. If the temperature increased 3 degrees each day until February 11, what is the range of the temperature for the week?

7. Tom buys school lunch for $2.50 every Monday, Wednesday, and Friday. If his mom writes a check at the beginning of the month, what is the total for all of his lunches in February?
   a. $2.50   c. $25.00
   b. $7.50   d. $30.00

8. Lisa's report about Rosa Parks was due on February 8. She turned it in on February 11. Her teacher took off 3 points for each day it was late. How many points did she lose?

9. Jeremiah is going to be in the Presidents' Day play. He needs 12 days to memorize his lines. On what date will he need to start preparing?

10. The pattern for the pictures on each month of the pet calendar is dog, cat, dog. Which type of animal will be pictured on the May calendar?

Calendar Challenge

The Picture:

The picture is a calendar hanging on a refrigerator. It displays the month of February. Groundhog Day, Valentine's Day, and Presidents' Day are printed on the calendar.

Teacher Notes:

While most students know that calendars are used primarily to schedule events, show them the math in each calendar. When teaching calendar skills, point out the patterns in the calendar. The days of the week repeat every seven days; the months of the year repeat every 12 months. While the position of the first day of the month may shift from month to month, the dates will fall in a pattern based on the first date. For example, if February 1 is a Tuesday, February 8, 15, and 22 will also fall on Tuesdays. Explain that to find the date of the same day of the next week, students should add seven to the date.

Teach students calendar vocabulary. Distinguish between the *day* (day of the week) and the *date* (a number). A *month* is approximately the amount of time it takes for the moon to travel around Earth. A *year* is the amount of time it takes Earth to travel around the sun. Every year, it takes $365\frac{1}{4}$ days for Earth to travel around the sun. The $\frac{1}{4}$ of a day each year is compounded into one day every four years. This is why every four years, February 29 is added to the calendar. This is called a *leap year*.

Extension Activities:

1. Give students 10 minutes to write different ways to use a calendar. Some examples might be the monthly school lunch menu, after-school activities, sporting events, birthdays, holidays, etc. After 10 minutes, have students exchange papers. Go around the room and have each student name something from the list. Write each named item on the board or chart paper. If another student has the same item on his list, he should cross it off. After all students have had turns, the student with the most items remaining on her list wins a prize. Talk about all of the items students listed. Play again by asking places you would find a calendar or people who use calendars every day.

2. Turn the days of the week into math problems. At the beginning of math, ask a student today's date. Once the student has given a correct answer, have students write math riddles or number sentences that have the date as their answers. For example, if the date is the third, then students could write "9 - 6" or "the number of sides on a triangle."

3. Write the date on the board with students in the room. This is a great opportunity to get students involved! Students can help you spell the day of the week and the month. They can use their logical thinking skills by saying "Yesterday was ___, so today is ___."

4. Learn the days of the week and months of the year in Spanish.

File Edit View History Bookmarks Window Help

Wed 11:36 AM

http://www.kingsfoods.us.co

King's Food Store

King's Food Store

- Groceries
- Health & Beauty
- Home Supplies
- This Week's Ad

There are currently 13 items in your cart.

- Sign Out
- Check Out

| Save List Changes | Print List | Rename List | Delete List |

Mom's Grocery List

- ○ Images
- ● Aisles

Add to Cart

			Select All	Total
Aisle 4	Healthy Ohs! Cereal 100% Whole-Grain Oats	20.00 oz.	1 ◄► Delete	$4.19
Aisle 5	Captain Chip Cookies	15.00 oz.	2 ◄► Delete	On Sale! 2/$6.00
Aisle 8	Reward Paper Towels 165 Sheets per Roll	1.00 oz.	1 ◄► Delete	$1.89
Aisle 9	Peppy Powder with Color Keeper	65.00 oz.	1 ◄► Delete	$5.99
Aisle 9	Zipit Sandwich Bags	100 ct.	1 ◄► Delete	$3.19
Aisle 13	Whiff Peanut Butter, Chunky, Reduced-Fat	18.00 oz.	1 ◄► Delete	$1.99
Aisle 13	Tummy's Favorite Bagels, Pre-Sliced, 6 Count	15.00 oz.	1 ◄► Delete	$2.89
Aisle 13	Harold 100% Whole-Wheat Bread, Sliced	24.00 oz.	2 ◄► Delete	$2.98
Dairy	Kroft Cheddar Cheese Slices, 16 Count	12.00 oz.	1 ◄► Delete	$1.89
Dairy	Moe's Market-Fresh, 2% Reduced-Fat Milk, 1/2 Gallon	64.00 fl. oz.	1 ◄► Delete	$2.69
Aisle 13	Pucker's Grape Jelly	18.00 oz.	1 ◄► Delete	$1.99

Grocery Shopping

Use the on-line grocery list to answer the questions.

1. Mr. Jackson is making sub sandwiches as a reward for good behavior. If there are 32 students in Mr. Jackson's class and each student wants a slice of cheese on his sandwich, how much would the cheese for the party cost?

2. Benji bought all of the items on Mom's Grocery List. How many different aisles did he go to collect all of the items?
   a. 6   c. 10
   b. 8   d. 11

3. Marlow's mom realizes that she has gone over the week's grocery budget. She decides not to buy the most expensive item in the cart. Which item did she decide not to buy?

4. Leo noticed that the Captain Chip cookies are on sale if he buys 2 packages. If he buys 2 packages, how much does he pay for each package?

5. How much would it cost Barry to buy the ingredients needed to make a peanut butter and jelly sandwich?

6. Tomás asked his parents to buy 2 items for his school lunch. If the items are the same price, which pair of items did Tomás want?
   a. cereal and jelly
   b. peanut butter and jelly
   c. sandwich bags and bread

7. Mrs. Fox uses 2 sandwich bags every day for each of her 2 sons. If she packs them lunch 5 days a week, how many weeks will a box of sandwich bags last?

8. Vanessa needs 1 pound of peanut butter to make a pie for her friend's birthday. How many jars of peanut butter will she need to buy to make the pie?

9. Josh compared prices at local bakeries and grocery stores for a loaf of Harold wheat bread. The best price he found was $3.50. How much less would he pay at King's Food Store for the same loaf?

10. Sierra wants to make a cake. The recipe calls for 2 cups of milk. If Sierra buys a half-gallon of milk, how many cups of milk will be left after she makes the recipe?

Name _____

Grocery Shopping

Use the on-line grocery list to answer the questions.

1. Karen needs to write a check to pay for the groceries on the list. What is the total that she will write on the check?

2. James and Anna made a batch of macaroni and cheese. If it takes 4 slices of cheese to make 1 serving, how many servings can they make with 1 package of cheese?

3. Lila has been keeping track of the average price of grocery items for 2 weeks. What is the average price of the items this week?

4. Charles added 1 more jar of jelly, another box of cookies, and another jar of peanut butter to the cart. How much was his total?

5. To save money, Harry decided to only buy only 1 of each item in the cart. What was his total cost?

6. Kris used 1 paper towel to clean up soda he spilled. About how much does 1 paper towel cost?
   a. 1¢   c. 10¢
   b. 5¢   d. 15¢

7. Jerry usually buys bagels at a local deli for 75¢ each. How much money will he save by buying them at King's?

8. Sophie's dad likes to know how much he is spending per ounce on food. What is the cost per ounce of Captain Chip Cookies?

9. Jackie spent 10 minutes in the store buying all of the items. What percentage of time did she spent in aisle 9?
   a. 2%   c. 14%
   b. 9%   d. 18%

10. What is the median price of the items on Mom's Grocery List?

11. How many item prices on the list are greater than the price of 1 package of Captain Chip cookies?

12. Ricardo's mom usually spends $50.00 per week on groceries. How much less did she spend on groceries this week?

Grocery Shopping

The Picture:

The picture is a grocery store Web site. It tells the following information about each item: aisle number, item name, size, quantity, and price.

Teacher Notes:

On-line shopping is becoming more widespread. Many grocery stores have Web sites on which shoppers can print out their lists before shopping in the store. For a minimal fee, other stores have employees who will shop for a customer and have the groceries ready to pick up.

Have students look for key words that determine which operation to use to solve word problems.
- Addition: *add, how many, combine, total, altogether, increase, sum*
- Subtraction: *less, fewer, how many more, left, decreased by, minus, difference*
- Multiplication: *number of times, product, multiple, each*
- Division: *per, each, quotient, percent*

Explain how to convert decimals to fractions and percents:
- Fraction to a decimal: Divide the numerator by the denominator.
- Decimal to a fraction: Remove the decimal point and write the number as the numerator. The denominator should be a multiple of 10, depending on the place the last digit of the decimal occupies. For example, if the decimal is 0.235, then the denominator is 1,000 because the last digit of the decimal occupies the thousandths place. The fraction can then be reduced to lowest terms.
- Fraction to a percent: Divide the numerator by the denominator, then move the decimal point two places to the right.
- Decimal to a percent: Move the decimal two places to the right.

Extension Activities:

1. Have students collect newspaper circulars for several local grocery stores. Give them a list of grocery items and let them determine if any are on sale in the circulars. Challenge students to find the best price for each item.
2. Tell students to ask local grocers if they participate in on-line grocery shopping programs. If they do, have students bring in the Web addresses and information about the programs. Let students use the classroom computer or visit the computer lab to practice navigating the sites.
3. Have students predict how much their families pay for groceries each month. Then, have students visit grocery stores with their families or have adults keep receipts. Post students' family sizes, predictions, and actual totals on a bulletin board.
4. Provide a short grocery list for students to price items at grocery stores. Then, have students visit grocery stores with adults. Have students price name-brand items and comparable store-brand items. Let students share the information with the class, then record the results on a graph.

Earl's DINER

• Open 7 Days a Week •
• Monday - Thursday 8 A.M. - 8 P.M. •
• Friday - Saturday 8 A.M. - 10 P.M. •
• Sunday 8 A.M. - 3 P.M. •

Soup

	cup	bowl
Vegetable	$1.00	$2.00
Cream of Broccoli	$1.00	$2.00
Chicken Noodle	$1.00	$2.00

Dessert

Brownie with Ice Cream	$2.00
Chocolate Chip Cookies (3)	$0.75
Carrot Cake	$1.00
Apple Pie...slice $2.00, whole pie $10.00	

Burgers
Served with fries
Fruit cup add 25¢

Hamburger	$3.00
Cheeseburger	$3.50
Bacon Cheeseburger	$4.00
Veggie Burger	$3.00

Drinks
Free refills

Soft Drinks	$1.00
Milk	$0.75
Tea	$1.00
Coffee	$0.75

Sandwiches
Served on your choice of bread
Choice of chips or fries
Fruit cup add 25¢

Ham & Cheese	$3.00
Tuna Fish	$3.00
Veggie Delight	$2.50
Grilled Cheese on White Toast	$2.00
Turkey & Cheese	$3.00

(served with lettuce, tomato, & mayo)

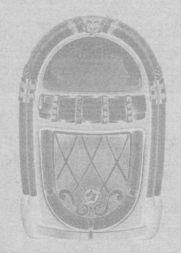

═══ **"Home of the biggest burgers in town."** ═══

Eat at Earl's Diner

Use the menu to answer the questions.

1. Angela went to Earl's Diner for lunch. She ordered a bowl of soup and a glass of milk. She paid with a $5.00 bill. How much change did she receive?

2. Matthew works at Earl's Diner on the weekends and earns $6.00 an hour. How much money will Matthew make if he works all day Sunday?

3. Jamie has 2 $1.00 bills, 3 quarters, 4 dimes, and 6 nickels. How much more money does she need to buy a hamburger and a soft drink?
   a. 65¢   c. 55¢
   b. 50¢   d. 45¢

4. Mary Ann would like to order a bowl of soup and a burger. How many different combinations could she order?

5. Randy, Sandy, and Mandy shared an order of chocolate chip cookies. If they each paid for 1 cookie, how much did each person spend?

6. Mr. Gray and 3 friends met for coffee. Mr. Gray paid for a cup of coffee for everyone. How much money did he spend altogether?

7. Mike spent $8.00 on apple pie. How many slices did he get?
   a. 1   c. 3
   b. 2   d. 4

8. Rosa bought a tuna fish sandwich, a fruit cup, and a soft drink. How much did she spend? How much change did she receive from a $5.00 bill?

9. Each pie has 8 slices. Tracie spent $6.00 on apple pie. What fraction of the pie did she buy?

10. Emilio wants to order a bowl of soup, a sandwich, a dessert, and a beverage. What is the least amount he could spend?

11. Tara paid $10.00 for lunch for her and a friend. If they split a brownie for dessert, what fraction of the price was the brownie?

Eat at Earl's Diner

Use the menu to answer the questions.

1. Steven likes chips more than fries. What fraction of burgers and sandwiches are served with a choice of chips or fries?

2. Darcy loved the piece of pie so much that she ordered a whole pie to take home. If the whole pie serves 8 people, how much does it cost per slice?
   a. $1.00   c. $1.50
   b. $1.25   d. $2.00

3. Van, Mary, and Kelly went to the diner together. They each ordered a cheeseburger and a soft drink. They split an order of cookies. If the bill was divided equally, how much did each person owe?

4. The longest shift a waiter at Earl's Diner works is 6 hours. If 1 waiter comes in every hour, how many waiters are there at closing time on Sunday?
   a. 5   c. 7
   b. 6   d. 8

5. Ted wanted to buy burgers for his ball team. He bought 9 of the same kind of burger and spent $31.50. What type of burger did he buy?

6. Jesper's mom is a waitress at Earl's Diner. She works from opening until closing on Sunday. If she averages $9.25 per hour, how much does she make on Sunday?

7. Payton bought 1 soup, 1 sandwich, 1 single-serving dessert, and 1 drink. If she bought the most expensive items, how much change would she receive from a $20.00 bill?

8. Tommy brought all of his allowance to Earl's Diner to pay for lunch. He has 1 $5.00 bill, 2 $1.00 bills, 3 quarters, and 2 dimes. He buys a bacon cheeseburger, a soft drink, and a cup of soup. How much more money does he need to buy a slice of pie?

9. Maggie cannot decide what she wants on her tuna fish sandwich. She has several topping choices. How many different ways can Maggie have her sandwich on wheat bread?

10. Tim works the first 5 hours the Diner is open on Tuesday. He earns $5.25 an hour. How many Tuesdays will he need to work to earn $189.00?

Eat at Earl's Diner

The Picture:
The picture is a menu from Earl's Diner. There are five categories of menu items. A price is listed to the right of each item. The diner's hours are also listed.

Teacher Notes:
Demonstrate possible combinations (number of ways to arrange different objects without repeating the same object) by making a list. Teach students with the following example:

How many possible combinations of three can be made with items A, B, C, and D?

1. Starting with the first variable (A), have students list all possible combinations by using the order of the items.
    - ABC
    - ABD
      (ACB is the same as ABC, just in a different order, so it is not counted.)
    - ACD
    (ADB is the same as ABD, just in a different order, so it is not counted.)
    (ADC is the same as ACD, just in a different order, so it is not counted.)
2. Have students count the distinct combinations on the list to find the answer. There are three possible combinations.

The most critical strategy for adding and subtracting money is lining up the decimal points. Teach students to line up decimals to correctly figure totals or change.

When making change, have students practice counting up to the next dollar. For example, if a student has a problem such as $5.00 - $1.37 = ?, have him count up three pennies to $1.40, a dime to $1.50, and then another 50¢ to $2.00. From this point, have him add dollars until he gets to $5.00.

Extension Activities:
1. Have students bring in a variety of paper menus from local restaurants. After giving students a budget, have them determine how many combinations of meals they can order from each menu.
2. Have students choose what items they would like to eat from Earl's Diner. Then, have them determine what the total bill would be for the class.
3. Let students create their own menus for a homework assignment. They should include on the menus the restaurants' names, logos, and menu items with various prices assigned. Post the menus on a bulletin board and use a different menu each day to incorporate into a mini math lesson at the start of each math class.
4. Invite a restaurant manager to talk to the class about how he uses math every day in his job. He should talk about customer counts, food orders, and menu prices versus the cost of food and labor.

Garden A
Garden B
Garden C
Garden D
fountain

20'
15'
10'
5'
0'

0' 5' 10' 15' 20' 25' 30'

1 ft. = 0.3 m

■ = planted area

© Carson-Dellosa • CD-104024

Planning a Garden

Use the garden plan to answer the questions.

1. After Mr. Rake measures the length and the width of his entire garden, he can figure the area. What is the total area of the entire garden?

2. Mr. Rake wants to landscape the garden. To make it easier, he divided the garden into 4 separate gardens. What is the area of 1 of the small gardens?

3. Because Mr. Rake needed to have water near his plants to water them, he built a fountain with a water spigot. What is the area of the fountain in the center of the garden?

4. To make it easier to water and care for his small gardens, Mr. Rake built paths between them. If each square unit is 1 meter, how many meters is the longest path from the edge of the garden to the edge of the fountain?
   a. 4   c. 13
   b. 8   d. 24

5. Half of Mr. Rake's yard is used for his entire garden. What is the total area of Mr. Rake's yard?

6. When boxwood bushes mature, they can be shaped by pruning them. What 20-foot^2 shape is Mr. Rake planning to make in garden A with his boxwoods?
   a. square   c. pentagon
   b. rectangle   d. hexagon

7. Gardens C and B both have triangles on opposite sides. If the triangles are congruent, how many square units are in all 4 triangles?

8. In each of the 4 gardens, the shaded area is reserved for plants and the lighter area is for soil and mulch. What area of garden A will be planted?

9. The brick mason needs to know the area for the entire path before he delivers the bricks for the path. If each square unit is equal to one meter, how many square meters is the entire path?

10. How many lines of symmetry does the entire garden have?

Planning a Garden

Use the garden plan to answer the questions.

1. Mr. Rake wants to put a fence around the entire garden to keep out animals. What is the perimeter of garden, including gates for the paths?
   a. 50 feet   c. 100 feet
   b. 60 feet   d. 600 feet

2. Mr. Rake has decided to make 2 pairs of congruent gardens. Which 2 gardens will have the same area covered with plants?
   a. A and B   c. B and D
   b. B and C   d. C and D

3. Half of Mr. Rake's yard is used for his entire garden. What is the perimeter of Mr. Rake's yard if one side is 30 meters wide?

4. Mr. Rake needs more water for the garden with the most plants. About how many more square meters are covered with plants in garden A than garden B?
   a. 3   c. 11
   b. 7   d. 13

5. Mr. Rake was describing his entire garden to a friend. Is garden C a reflection, rotation, or translation of garden A?

6. Mr. Rake's favorite subject in school was math. He became a geometric garden planner. His favorite angles are right angles. How many right angles are there in the planted area garden D?

7. Because Mr. Rake had so many right angles in his garden, he decided to add obtuse angles in garden D. How many obtuse angles did he use in the planted part of garden D?

8. Mr. Rake noticed that he did not have any acute angles in gardens A and D, so he added some acute angles to the other 2 gardens. How many acute angles are there in the planted sections of gardens B and C?

9. Mr. Rake paid $3.00 for each square foot that he planted in his garden. How much did he pay for all of the plants in the garden?

10. Mr. Rake decided to make his garden larger. Instead of measuring each square unit in feet, he used meters. If the garden is 20' x 30', what is the perimeter in meters?

Planning a Garden

The Picture:

The picture is a blueprint for a garden. There is a fountain in the center, and four intersecting paths meet at the fountain. Each shaded square represents one square foot of planted area. Light areas are dirt or mulch areas. There are four gardens that are labeled A-D. Gardens A and D are congruent, and gardens B and C are congruent. There is a number grid on the x- and y-axis to make counting easier.

Teacher Notes:

Teach students to find the area of a garden, planted area, or path by counting the number of squares it contains. Explain that two triangles equal one square unit. When trying to find an area within another area, have students find the area of the entire garden, then subtract the area of a given planted area. The difference is the remaining area of the garden.

Teach students to find perimeter by counting the number of units around the outside of a figure.

Tell students that a simple way to remember the difference between area and perimeter is *area* rhymes with "squarea," which should tell them to find square units. Then, introduce the prefix *peri-* as meaning "around." Therefore, *perimeter* means "the meters around." To remember *perimeter*, tell students that it could mean to find the meters around the outside.

When teaching students about angles, give them word associations to remember the difference between the types of angles.
- For a right angle, have students hold their arms straight out at their shoulders so that their bodies make Ts. Tell students that this is a line, not an angle. To make a right angle, each student should hold her left arm straight out to the side , parallel to the floor, and hold her right arm "right" against her right ear.
- For an acute angle, students should move their arms touching their ears across their faces to simulate alligators' jaws. Explain that an acute angle covers the "cute" face.
- Finally, students should move their arms back across their faces and angle them so that their arms resemble the hour hand on a clock in the two o'clock position. Explain that obtuse is "on two."

Extension Activities:
1. Give each student a piece of graph paper. Have her create two congruent gardens that have four planted areas inside. After students have created their garden blueprints, have them figure out the areas and perimeters of their gardens. Then, give students a price list for different plants. Have them choose a variety of plants to place in their gardens while staying on a pre=determined budget.
2. Encourage students to adopt a community garden in the school's neighborhood. Students can help create a neighborhood garden if there is not one in existence. Make sure students' plans for the neighborhood garden accommodate people with special needs.
3. Download aerial views of gardens from the Internet. Have students identify different shapes and angles in each garden.

Geoboard
Top 10 Hits

This Week	Last Week	Weeks on Chart	Title Artist	Peak Position
1	1	10	**Quotient in Motion** The Dividends	1
2	2	14	**That's Alright Angle** The Triangles	2
3	3	10	**Pi in the Sky** Celestial Circle	3
4	5	10	**Oops! I Added Again** Sum Band	4
5	6	19	**Too Much Information** Extraneous	4
6	8	6	**We Are Congruent** Equal-A-Tee	6
7	7	17	**Why Must You Go Away?** Powers of Subtraction	1
8	4	8	**Are We Symmetric When We Are Apart?** The Reflections	4
9	10	15	**The Point of the Pyramid** Polly Hedron	2
10	9	5	**Getting Even** The Odd Squad	4

Top of the Charts

Use the music chart to answer the questions.

1. Geoboard gives a framed CD cover to each group that has a number 1 hit. How many bands on the chart this week will receive framed CD covers?

2. Carla bought the CD with the song that has been in the Top 10 the longest. Which artist's CD did Carla buy?

3. How many more weeks has "Why Must You Go Away?" been on the Top 10 chart than "Getting Even"?

4. How many songs on the chart this week have not changed positions from last week?

5. The music store buys fewer CDs from recording companies who have songs that lose positions on the chart. How many songs have dropped positions this week?
   a. 1   c. 3
   b. 2   d. 4

6. What fraction of the songs on the chart this week have been in the top 5 of the Geoboard Top 10?

7. What is the total number of weeks the top 5 songs have been on the Top 10 list?

8. What fraction of the songs on the chart have been on the chart for fewer than 10 weeks?
   a. $\frac{7}{10}$ c. $\frac{2}{5}$
   b. $\frac{3}{10}$ d. $\frac{1}{2}$

9. If "We Are Congruent" moves up the chart 4 positions next week, what number would it be on the chart?

10. The band Extraneous started touring 2 weeks after their song hit the Top 10. How many weeks have they been touring?

11. Celestial Circle has sold 1 million copies of their CD every week they have been on the Top 10 chart. If they sold each CD for $15.00, how much money did they make?
    a. $1 million   c. $15 million
    b. $10 million   d. $150 million

Top of the Charts

Use the music chart to answer the questions.

1. People all over the world hear songs when radio stations play them. Many stations play Top 10 songs. Which Top 10 bands' songs have been heard on the radio for more than 10 weeks?

2. Because the Top 10 is determined by listeners, many bands change positions every week. Which band on the chart this week was fourth on the chart last week?

3. A record producer is looking for bands that have had hits in the Top 10 for several weeks. What is the average number of weeks the songs on this week's list have been in the Top 10?

4. Many songs change positions in the Top 10. What is the mode of the peak position column on the Top 10 chart?

5. Polly Hedron's song was just released to radio stations in Canada. She now has many new fans. What is the range of positions for her hit song?
   a. 1   c. 9
   b. 8   d. 10

6. The Reflections have released their next big hit. It is number 27 on the chart, so their current Top 10 hit is slipping. How many places did "Are We Symmetric When We Are Apart?" fall on the chart this week?
   a. 4   c. 12
   b. 8   d. 20

7. According to information on this week's chart, what fraction of the weeks that "Pi in the Sky" has been in the Top 10 has it been number 3 on the chart?

8. Becky's favorite band is Extraneous. David's favorite band is Powers of Subtraction. According to the chart, which band has been more popular on the Geoboard chart?

9. The Triangles are going on tour to help sell their new CD. They are touring with an artist that has been on the Top 10 chart one week longer than they have. Which other artist is on their tour?

Top of the Charts

The Picture:

The picture is a chart of the Top 10 hits for one week. The chart shows the positions in the current week's order. Additional information provided is the position held by each song last week, the number of weeks a song has been on the Top 10 chart, each song's name followed by the artist who performs it, and the peak or top position the song has held in the Top 10.

Teacher Notes:

Explain that the Top 10 hits are determined by the number of song requests radio stations receive and the results of audience surveys. Because the hits are determined by audiences, they fluctuate from week to week.

Have students determine range by finding the difference between the largest and smallest numbers in a set.

Make sure students read the questions carefully before deciding what operation to use. Encourage them to underline important information and to cross out extraneous information.

Extension Activities:

1. Have students vote on which songs they like to listen to and record the information. Then, let them survey random students from different grade levels and compare the information on a graph. Have students brainstorm why preferences are similar or different.
2. Using the data gathered from the previous activity, have students make a Top 10 chart for the school.
3. Let students compare the school's Top 10 chart to a national chart. Help them determine what fraction of the songs on the school's Top 10 chart are on the national chart.
4. Have students search the Internet for a current list of top 10 children's books. Let them predict if the books will move up or down the list in the next week. Assign titles from the list to small groups of students to track over the next few months. Students can make line graphs to show each book's progress.
5. Play world music for students. Discuss how these songs are similar to or different from songs on the school's Top 10 chart. As you play each song, let students guess its country of origin. Tell students the correct country if necessary and have a volunteer mark the song on a world map with a pushpin and a self-stick note with the song's name.

AMBER CINEMA 6 • 555-2341

142 Olefin Road
Corner of I-95 and I-24

LUCK & MONEY (R)
1:00, 3:00, 5:00, 7:00, 9:00

THE ART OF PEACE (PG-13)
7:15, 9:00

SPACESTORM (PG)
5:20, 7:30, 9:40

TECHNOHAZARD II (R)
1:15, 3:15, 5:15, 7:15, 9:15

MEET THE DOOLUSKYS (G)
1:10, 2:45, 4:20, 5:55

BACK ROAD (PG)
3:00, 5:00, 7:00, 9:00

All shows before 6:00 P.M.
are $5.75. After 6:00 P.M.,
seats are $8.50.

RIDGEVILLE THEATER 3

555-5549 • 422 Main Street
Next to Nora's Flower Shop

THE DARK FOREST (PG-13)
6:35, 8:00

A DOG, A CAT, AND A DONKEY (G)
1:00, 2:30, 4:00, 5:30, 7:00

SPACESTORM (PG)
5:05, 7:15, 9:25

All shows before 6:30 P.M. are $5.25.
After 6:30 P.M., seats are $8.75.
Ages 10 and under: $4.75 all day

G = All audiences
PG = Parents should be aware of
content before deciding whether
children should view the movie.
PG-13 = Children under 13 are
not admitted without a parent or
guardian.
R = No one under 17 is admitted
without a parent or guardian.

RBW Woodbridge Mall Cinema 7

THE FRIENDLY WIZARD (G)
1:00*, 3:00, 5:00, 7:00, 9:00

BENDER LAKE (PG)
3:15, 5:15, 7:15

GET ON THE ROAD (PG)
1:00*, 5:00, 9:00

THE ARTISTS (R)
5:15, 7:15, 9:15, 11:15

TECHNOHAZARD II (R)
7:30, 9:30

BACK ROAD (PG)
3:00, 5:00, 7:00, 9:00

A DOG, A CAT, AND A DONKEY (G)
12:30+, 2:00, 3:30

+ Special $1.00 Show * Special $2.00 Show

All shows before 6:00 P.M. are $5.75. All shows after 6:00 P.M. are $8.00.

293 Towne Avenue • 555-6155 • www.regaliacinemas.com

Sharps Cinema 4

Supersaver Matinee for adults **$6.00**
(all shows before 5:00 P.M.)

221 Westpoint Road • 555-9901

SPACESTORM (PG)
5:20, 7:30, 9:40, 11:50

CIRCUS RING (R)
7:45, 10:00

MEET THE DOOLUSKYS (G)
2:45, 4:20, 5:55

BENDER LAKE (PG)
3:30, 5:30, 7:30, 9:30

Regular Show Price after 5:00 P.M.
Adults: $9 Children (12 and under): $5

Let's Go to the Movies

Use the movie listings to answer the questions.

1. Barbara decides to take her 11-year-old son to see *Bender Lake*. It is 3:00 P.M., and it takes 20 minutes to get to either theater showing the movie. If they want to arrive before the movie starts, which theater should they choose?

2. Barbara likes to save money, so she is going to the early movie. How much will Barbara pay for 1 adult and 1 child ticket for the 3:30 showing of *Bender Lake*?

3. Marion was happy to find out that the movies she wanted to see was playing in most local theaters. What fraction of the movie theaters is showing *Spacestorm*?

4. It's 5:30 P.M., and Wyatt and his friend Tana want to go see a movie before 6:00 P.M. To get the best price, which theater should they go to?

5. What is the total price for 5 tickets to *The Art of Peace*?

6. All theaters in the city of Ridgeville advertise their movies and show times in *The Tellall Post*. How many movie theaters are in Ridgeville?

7. All movies advertised have come out in the last 3 weeks. How many movies are showing?

8. Tyson prefers a movie theater with a variety of show times. How many more show times does the Woodbridge Mall Cinema have than Ridgeville Theater?

9. Kaitlin was home from the theater 15 minutes after the movie ended. She paid $5.75 for her ticket to *The Artists*, a 2-hour movie. What time did she get home from the theater?

10. Julio is comparing prices to save money. Which costs more, 4 tickets for an after 6:30 P.M. showing at Ridgeville Theater or 3 tickets for an evening showing at Sharps Cinema?

11. What fraction of movies at Woodbridge Mall cinema are shown before 6:00 P.M.?

12. Mrs. Fox took her children, John, Elizabeth, and Isabel to see the matinee of Meet the Dooluskys at the Amber Cinema. How much did it cost for their tickets?

Name _____

Let's Go to the Movies

Use the movie listings to answer the questions.

1. The Hanson family went to see *A Dog, A Cat, and A Donkey* at 5:30 P.M. They paid $21.00. How many people are in the Hanson family?

2. Cliff and his brother Stan paid $18.00 for tickets to see an R-rated movie. What movie did they see?

3. The McCluskey family has 8 children. They are always looking for special prices so that they can see movies as a family. Which movie would be the least expensive for them to see? How much would they spend?

4. Movies are rated according to content. Movie companies can make more money on children's movies because the children must attend with adults. If you count each title once, about what percentage of the movies showing are rated G, PG, or PG-13?
   a. 10%   c. 69%
   b. 15%   d. 75%

5. Mrs. Spencer took all of the children in her neighborhood to a movie. How much are 20 tickets to the first showing of *The Friendly Wizard*?

6. Mr. and Mrs. Lance have 4 children under 10 years old. How much money will they save on tickets for their family of 6 by going to see *Spacestorm* at the Ridgeville Theater 5:05 P.M. show time rather than the 5:20 P.M. show time at Sharps Cinema?

7. A teacher took some of his fourth-grade students to see the 2:45 P.M. showing of *Meet the Dooluskys*. He paid the lowest price of $55.00 for students' tickets. How many students went to the movie?

8. Eric took his best friend to see a movie for his 18th birthday. Eric paid $10.50 for 2 tickets. Which movie could they be watching?
   a. *Circus Ring*
   b. *Meet the Dooluskys*
   c. *The Dark Forest*
   d. *The Art of Peace*

9. Gwyneth is a Cliff Westward fan. She wants to be one of the first people in town to see his new movie, so she gets in line an hour before the movie starts. Where and when will Gwyneth be at the theater?

Let's Go to the Movies

The Picture:

The picture is a newspaper page that contains movie listings. There are two advertisements for movies and a rating system chart. The four cinemas listed each give movie titles, show times, and prices.

Teacher Notes:

Explain that when a person plans to see a movie, there are several factors she must take into account. First, a person chooses which movie to see, then she finds a theater that is showing that movie. Next, she chooses the time to see the movie. Price may also be a factor when choosing the time of the movie because most theaters have discounts for early show times, which are also called matinees.

When students compare prices, theaters, and show times, have them create charts to make it easier to cross-reference information. If movie titles and ratings are being compared, make sure that students count each title only once.

Stress the importance of reading problems carefully before beginning the problem-solving process. Have students cross out extraneous information, then choose which operation to use. Have them choose the best problem-solving strategy from the following list:

- Find a pattern.
- Make a table or a list.
- Work backward.
- Guess and check (for multiple choice).
- Draw a picture.
- Write a number sentence.

Extension Activities:

1. Plan a class trip to the movies or a performance, such as a concert or play. Have students determine how many cars are needed to transport the class.
2. Plan a field trip with the class. Have students calculate the cost of transportation using a bus.
3. Obtain a variety of advertisements for movies, plays, or concerts in your area. Have students compare costs and determine which is the best buy.
4. Have students write persuasive letters to the manager of a movie theater asking for free tickets to a specific movie that is approved by the school administration and families.
5. Make a bar graph or pictograph of students' favorite movies.

TERRIFIC 5–DAY FORECAST

Monday	Tuesday	Wednesday	Thursday	Friday
80°F/27°C	88°F/31°C	90°F/32°C	92°F/33°C	95°F/35°C
	69°F/20°C	69°F/20°C	70°F/21°C	73°F/23°C

NATION

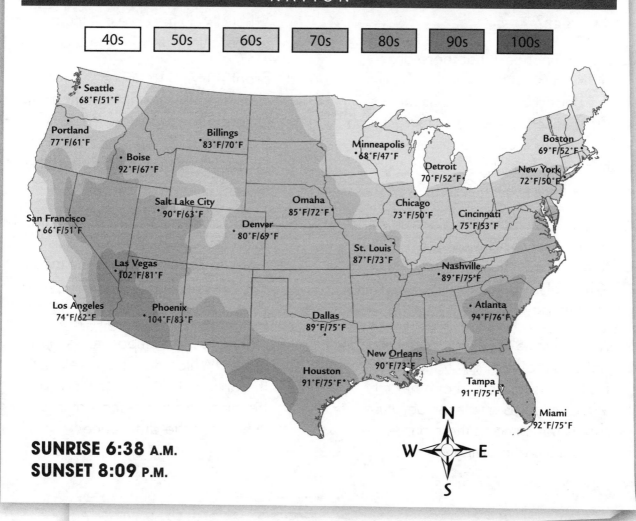

40s 50s 60s 70s 80s 90s 100s

Seattle 68°F/51°F
Portland 77°F/61°F
Boise 92°F/67°F
Billings 83°F/70°F
Minneapolis 68°F/47°F
Boston 69°F/52°F
Detroit 70°F/52°F
New York 72°F/50°F
Salt Lake City 90°F/63°F
Omaha 85°F/72°F
Chicago 73°F/50°F
Cincinnati 75°F/53°F
San Francisco 66°F/51°F
Denver 80°F/69°F
St. Louis 87°F/73°F
Nashville 89°F/75°F
Las Vegas 102°F/81°F
Los Angeles 74°F/62°F
Phoenix 104°F/83°F
Dallas 89°F/75°F
Atlanta 94°F/76°F
New Orleans 90°F/73°F
Houston 91°F/75°F
Tampa 91°F/75°F
Miami 92°F/75°F

SUNRISE 6:38 A.M.
SUNSET 8:09 P.M.

Weather Watch

Use the weather map to answer the questions.

1. Martrina lives in the city of Terrific. According to *The Terrific Times*, how long will the sun be up today?

2. Chester noticed a wide difference in the weather this week. What is the difference in °F between Terrific's hottest high temperature of the week and the lowest high temperature of the week?

3. Kendall noticed that there are differences in the weather across the United States. What is the difference between the lowest high temperature and the greatest high temperature in °F? What cities have these temperatures?

4. Kendall noticed that, on average, northern cities have cooler temperatures than southern cities. Which city has the lowest temperature for Monday?

5. Montel lives in Billings, Montana. He noticed that the high temperature in his town is the low in another city. Which city has a low temperature that is the same as the high temperature in Billings?

6. Ilene is planning to fly across the country to San Francisco today. If San Francisco's high temperature is 3 degrees cooler than the high in her hometown, from which city will she be flying?

7. Maria is visiting her grandparents in the southwestern part of the country. What city do they live in if the average temperature today will be 68°F?

8. Brent is trying to figure out what clothes to wear on his flight from Chicago to Las Vegas. What is the difference between the high temperature for Chicago and the high temperature for Las Vegas?

9. Horacio's pen pal asked him what the average low temperature was this week in Terrific. What is the mean low temperature in °C for the week?

10. Monique was looking at the nighttime low temperatures in the paper. Which day this week had the greatest difference between the high and low temperatures in °F? What was the difference?

Weather Watch

Use the weather map to answer the questions.

1. Joan noticed a wide range in the temperature in the Terrific 5-day forecast. What is the difference in °C between the highest temperature of the week and the lowest temperature of the week?

2. Sandra rides in the backseat with her brother during her family's trip from Atlanta to New York. They are leaving on Monday when the sun comes up and will arrive $2\frac{1}{2}$ hours after the sun goes down. How long will they drive?

3. Renée is thinking about moving to Terrific. She has *The Terrific Times* sent to her home in Atlanta to learn about the weather there. What is the average high temperature in °F in Terrific's 5-day forecast?

4. What percentage of the cities on the map have high temperatures in the 60s on Monday?
   a. 10%   c. 16%
   b. 24%   d. 28%

5. Many cities have extreme differences in temperature in a single day. Which city west of Denver has the widest range between the high and low temperatures for the day?

6. What percentage of the cities on the map are not in the 100°F range on Monday?

7. Pen pals Melinda and Hallie are chatting on the computer. Melinda lives in Portland. Hallie lives in Houston. What are the mean of the high temperatures and the mean of the low temperatures in their 2 cities?
   a. 91°F and 68°F
   b. 81.5°F and 71°F
   c. 84°F and 68°F

8. What is the average high temperature for all cities in which the high reaches 80°F or higher?

9. What is the median low temperature of all cities on the map?

10. What percentage of the cities on the map will have a high of at least 90°F for the day?

Weather Watch

The Picture:
The picture is a national weather map and a weekly local forecast from a newspaper called *The Terrific Times*. The local temperatures shown are in Fahrenheit and Celsius. The local high temperature for each day is listed under the picture of the weather conditions. The nighttime lows are listed between the days of the week. The national weather map lists certain cities and their highs and lows in degrees Fahrenheit. The shading shows dark areas for high temperatures and light areas for low temperatures throughout the country.

Teacher Notes:
Tell students that people rely on weather forecasts when making plans for the day and even the week. Weather reports also let people know when they should water plants and help people decide what clothes to wear. Many people rely on weather reports to do their jobs. For example, farmers rely on the weather for good crops, and people who work on computers watch for days where heavy lightning can zap computers!

People who predict the weather are called *meteorologists*. They use computers and mathematical equations to predict the weather.

Extension Activities:
1. Talk about kinds of storms and which areas are most affected. For example, the U.S. states of Louisiana, Arkansas, Missouri, Nebraska, Texas, Kansas, and Oklahoma, and the Canadian province of New Brunswick are known to have hundreds of tornadoes every year. These storms are tracked by storm chasers who use mathematical equations to determine where the next storm will be. They also use this information to warn people that a tornado is coming. Snowstorms are common in the northern U.S. states, while in parts of Florida people can often wear swimsuits in December!
2. Talk about what weather conditions are best for certain activities. Then, have students draw pictures of themselves participating in outdoor activities and write what the temperature would be outside for those activities.
3. Have a meteorologist come to your school or visit a weather center in your area on a field trip.
4. Chart the weather for one month in your classroom. Note any patterns you find in the weather throughout the month.
5. Search the Internet to find out the times the sun will rise and set in your area. Create a graph to show how days become shorter from fall to winter and longer from winter to spring. Even though all days have 24 hours, the number of hours of daylight changes every day, making the days appear to be longer or shorter. Have students create a bar graph and ask if they notice a pattern. Ask if there are days in spring and fall with the same amount of daylight.

Jill's Famous Fruit Salad

1/3 apple, cored, peeled, and chopped

3/8 cup pineapple juice

1/2 banana, peeled and sliced

1/8 pineapple, cored, peeled, and sliced

1/2 orange, peeled and sectioned

3 strawberries, tops removed and sliced

1/4 cup pecan pieces

Put the banana and apple in a bowl. This and cover with pineapple juice. This will keep the fruit from darkening. Drain. Add the remaining ingredients. Toss gently.

(Makes 3 one-cup servings)

J & J's Fresh Lemonade

3 3/4 cups water

5 lemons, seeded and squeezed

1/2 cup sugar

Combine all ingredients and shake.

(Makes 5 one-cup servings)

Jim's Peanut Butter Bars

1 285-gram package mini marshmallows

2/3 cup peanut butter

1/2 cup butter

5 1/2 cups crisp rice cereal *

1 1/4 cups mini chocolate chips

Combine marshmallows, peanut butter, and butter in a saucepan. Heat on low and stir. Be careful—the mixture can easily burn. When melted, remove from stove. Add cereal and chips. Stir to combine. Place in 9" (23 cm) square pan. Cool.

* You may substitute other unsweetened cereals.

(Makes 9 huge bars)

Vegetable Soup

1 tablespoon olive oil

2 1/2 cups carrots, sliced

1 1/2 cups onion, diced

1 1/2 cups celery, cut into thin slices

12 cups chicken broth

1 1/4 cups string beans, cut to 1/2 inch

1/2 cup stewed tomatoes

3/4 cup zucchini, diced

1 tablespoon dried basil

Salt and pepper to taste.

Place olive oil in a Dutch oven. Add carrots, onion, and celery. Cook and stir until onion is golden. Add broth, string beans, and tomato paste. Stir well. Simmer for 15 minutes. Add the remaining ingredients. Simmer for 10 minutes. Serve hot.

(Makes 20 one-cup servings)

Cooking for a Crowd

Use the recipes to answer the questions.

1. Pedro is running for class president. His mom is preparing soup for everyone who is helping him make posters. To make 40 cups of vegetable soup, how many cups of diced onion will she need?

2. Tanya told Mrs. Montano that she will make soup at her house. If she is making 10 cups of vegetable soup, how much chicken broth will she need?

3. Uma needed 2 bags of mini marshmallows to make 2 batches of peanut butter bars. How many grams of mini marshmallows did Uma use to make 18 peanut butter bars?

4. Tommy is the team manager for his baseball team and provided drinks for the game last Saturday. He used 50 lemons to make some lemonade. How many cups of lemonade did he make?
   a. 20   c. 40
   b. 25   d. 50

5. Celia wants to earn money by having a lemonade stand. She wants to start by making 10 cups of lemonade. How much water will she need?

6. Becky will make 27 peanut butter bars for Sandra's slumber party this weekend. How many cups of rice cereal will she need to make 27 peanut butter bars?

7. Randy has never cooked before, so he made sure he carefully followed the directions on the recipe. If Randy followed the recipe exactly, how long would 1 side of 1 peanut butter bar be?

8. If Jill decides to change her recipe so that it makes 9 cups of fruit salad, which of these ingredient changes is correct?
   a. $\frac{1}{4}$ cup pineapple
   b. $\frac{1}{4}$ cup pecan pieces
   c. 1 apple
   d. 1 banana

9. There was a sale on fruit at the farmers' market. George decided to make fruit salad for a healthy snack. If he uses 12 strawberries to make fruit salad, how much fruit salad is he making?

CD-104024 • Real-World Math

Name _____

Cooking for a Crowd

Use the recipes to answer the questions.

1. For Lila's winter party, she needs to make enough vegetable soup so that each of her 60 guests can eat 1 cup. How many cups of chicken broth will she need to make the soup?

2. Virginia doubled the amount of her favorite vegetable in the vegetable soup. She used $2\frac{1}{2}$ cups instead of the recommended amount. What is Virginia's favorite vegetable?

3. After cutting up the vegetables for the soup, Billy added the total cups of vegetables he used in the recipe. About how many total cups of vegetables are required to make the vegetable soup?
   a. 2 cups   c. 12 cups
   b. 8 cups   d. 16 cups

4. Mischa's mom does not want her to have much sugar in her diet. Mischa loves fresh lemonade but can only drink it if it is less than 20% sugar. What percentage of a cup of sugar is in each cup of lemonade?

5. Jason is at a store buying the ingredients for lemonade. How much sugar will Jason need to make 25 cups of lemonade?

6. Joni's sister loves peanut butter bars. She was trying to figure out how many bars Joni was making by watching her add the peanut butter to the mix. If Joni used 2 cups of peanut butter, how many bars was she making?

7. How much larger is the amount of peanut butter than butter in Jim's Peanut Butter Bars?

8. Ling likes banana in her fruit salad. If she adds another whole banana to the fruit salad, how much more pineapple juice will she need to add?
   a. $\frac{3}{8}$ cup   c. $\frac{1}{2}$ cup
   b. $\frac{1}{4}$ cup   d. $\frac{3}{4}$ cup

9. Mrs. Maready is making 1 cup of lemonade for every cup of vegetable soup. How many batches of lemonade must she make to equal 1 batch of vegetable soup?

10. Jim made enough peanut butter bars for 18 people to each have 1. He made 3 times the number of batches of fruit salad than peanut butter bars. How many servings of fruit salad did he make?

Cooking for a Crowd

The Picture:

The picture is four different recipes: lemonade, vegetable soup, peanut butter bars, and fruit salad. Each recipe includes the amount of each ingredient needed, directions for making the recipe, and the number of servings the recipe makes.

Teacher Notes:

Familiarize students with the following recipe vocabulary:
- *batch*—the amount produced by preparing a recipe exactly as written
- *servings*—the number of portions recommended by the recipe
- *ingredients*—the individual parts combined to make a recipe
- *simmer*—to cook food gently in liquid at a low temperature so that tiny bubbles begin to break the surface

To make fractions equivalent, have students find the least common multiple of the two denominators. Tell them to remember the number each denominator was multiplied by in order to get the least common multiple. Then, have them multiply each numerator by the corresponding number.

Extension Activities:

1. Create a class cookbook. Have students bring in their favorite family recipes. Then, have students categorize the recipes into different courses or types of food, such as appetizers, vegetables, casseroles, etc. Help students alphabetize the recipes in each section by name and create a table of contents. Make copies of the table of contents and recipes and let each student design a cover for her cookbook. Send the cookbooks home with students.

2. Bring in whole fruits and have students estimate how many cups they will produce when cut into small pieces. When students have completed their estimates, help them cut the fruit with plastic knives and measure how many cups were produced. Have students compare this information with their estimates. Then, allow students to enjoy the cut fruit for a snack. (Before completing any food activity, get families' permission and inquire about students' allergies and religious or other food preferences.)

3. Invite restaurant cooks or the school's cafeteria manager to the classroom to talk about how they cook for many people in one day. Discuss how meals' prices reflect the cost of ingredients and the labor and utilities needed to prepare the food.

4. Use recipes to reinforce measurement conversion skills. Print several recipes from the Internet or copy them from cookbooks or magazines. Have students convert standard measurements to metric measurements and vice versa. Remind students that in addition to ingredient amounts, pan sizes, and oven temperatures should also be converted.

Greencroft Hills School
June Newsletter

Parents and kids—Don't miss out! During the month of June, three amusement parks are offering special rates. It is the perfect time of year to get family and friends together for thrilling rides, interesting shows, and family fun! We have listed the information below so that you can choose which park you might like to attend.

Daily Adventure Prices		Annual Adventure Prices	
Adult	$37.50	Adult	$120.50
Student	$29.95	Student	$100.95
Child Ages 2-10	$19.95	Child Ages 2-10	$95.95
Senior Ages 65+	$19.95	Senior Ages 65+	$95.95

Unlimited rides with the price of admission!

fun time
AMUSEMENT PARKS

Free admission in June.

Each ride is five tickets.
45-Ticket Book $20.00
30-Ticket Book $13.00
15-Ticket Book $7.00
Individual Ticket $0.50
Free cotton candy!
Buy your tickets now!

KING'S COURT

Ride all day for:
Adult	$35.00
Student	$30.00
Child (under 10)	$18.00
Senior (ages 65+)	$15.00

(Shows $5.00 Extra)

Special June Savings
Every student from Greencroft Hills School receives a free ice cream cone during the month of June!

Name _____

For Your Amusement

Use the newsletter to answer the questions.

1. To celebrate the last day of school, Debbie and Diane bought 2 student tickets to an amusement park. If they paid $60.00, for which park did they buy their tickets?

2. Margaret went to Fun Time Amusement Park with her friend. They each want to ride the 3 fastest rides. Which ticket book should they each buy?

3. As a graduation present, Dean's grandparents gave him 75 tickets to Fun Time Amusement Park. How many rides can Dean go on with the tickets he received?

4. Dean's sister graduated last year and received a student's pass to King's Court. How much more money did Dean's grandparents spend on his graduation present?

5. Cooper is always looking for a good deal. Ashley bought 15 individual tickets at Fun Time, and Cooper bought the 15-ticket book, how much more did Ashley spend?
   a. $0.50   c. $7.00
   b. $1.50   d. $7.50

6. Cole bought 30 tickets but had to buy more to ride all of the rides she wanted to ride. If Cole went on 9 rides and had no tickets left, how many tickets did she buy altogether?

7. Jolene bought 45 individual tickets. Lisa bought a 30-ticket book and a 15-ticket book. Who spent more money on her tickets?

8. Justin's grandfather loves going to amusement parks but he is on a fixed budget. If his grandfather goes to High Adventure 10 times during the month of June, how much money will he save by getting an annual pass?

9. If Amanda bought 3 books of 15 tickets, how many rides can she go on at Fun Time?

10. Kennedy has $25.00 to spend at Fun Time. If she buys a drink for $2.00 and a hot dog for $3.00, how many rides can she go on with the remaining money?
    a. 7   c. 9
    b. 8   d. 10

Name _____

For Your Amusement

Use the newsletter to answer the questions.

1. The Bell family includes 3 adults, 3 students, and 1 child. Which park would be the best deal for them, High Adventure or King's Court?

2. The Bell family went to High Adventure 5 times during their vacation. How much money would the Bell family have saved if they had purchased an annual pass to the park?

3. How many daily children's tickets did Mr. Cary buy at High Adventure if he paid $59.85?

4. Pete's family is celebrating his good report card. What is the lowest price Pete's family of 1 senior, 1 adult, and 2 students can pay for day passes to an amusement park?

5. The Wilsons want to know the average price of a child's ticket for a day at High Adventure or King's Court. What is the average price of a child's ticket?
   a. $18.00   c. $19.95
   b. $18.98   d. $95.95

6. The Johnson family bought 3 tickets for High Adventure Theme Park. The average price for the tickets was $31.65. What tickets did they buy?

7. Monte wanted to see a show at King's Court. Two of his friends decided to come along. How much did Monte and his friends pay for show tickets?

8. The Hassel family is trying to figure out which package would be best for them at High Adventure. They plan to go to the park 3 times in June. If they need 2 adult tickets, 1 senior ticket, and 2 child tickets, which is the best package for them, daily or annual?

9. What would the High Adventure annual price be for 2 adults, 3 students, 1 child, and 0 seniors?

10. Mark is 10 years old. He has a younger sister who wants to go to King's Court. How much will it cost for the 2 of them to go with their father?
    a. $95.00   c. $71.00
    b. $88.00   d. $83.00

For Your Amusement

The Picture:

The picture is a June Newsletter for Greencroft Hills School. The school is receiving special prices at three amusement parks. Two advertisements include prices for each age group while the other lists prices per ticket.

Teacher Notes:

Key information for one problem may be found in a previous problem. Encourage students to use previous information and solutions to solve other problems.

Before making price comparisons among theme parks, students should evaluate individual prices. For example, at Fun Times Amusement Park it is less expensive to purchase one 30-ticket book for $13.00 than to purchase two 15-ticket books for a total of $14.00.

Extension Activities:

1. Have students compare the admission prices and special rates of amusement parks in their area.
2. Let students work in teams to design models of theme park rides using common or recycled materials. Tell students that each ride should have a mechanical working part. When complete, display the theme park rides. Note: Some communities have Theme Park Challenge competitions for elementary school students. Check with your local engineering society for details.
3. Have students work with partners to develop price plans for amusement parks. Have students:
    *   Decide if they want to visit the park for a full day or a half-day.
    *   Decide if they will visit with their families or with the class and determine the cost.
    *   Compare the cost of each group's plan.
4. To integrate geometry, have students make posters of theme park rides that include several geometric shapes.
5. Volunteer your class to plan a carnival to raise money for the school. Obtain a budget from the school's administration. Then, help students decide on ticket prices and rides, games, prizes, and activities to feature. Use this opportunity to teach students how to work within a provided budget. Once the plan is approved by the school's administration, have students enlist families to make food to sell, such as caramel apples, cotton candy, and other foods commonly found at amusement parks. Have students create posters and flyers to advertise the carnival and solicit volunteers to help sell tickets, run game booths, etc.

Bone Voyage
Canine Camp

Time	Activity
6:00 A.M. – 8:00 A.M.	Breakfast
8:00 A.M. – 9:30 A.M.	Nature Hike
9:30 A.M. – 10:30 A.M.	Swimming (lessons optional)
10:30 A.M. – 11:00 A.M.	Finding Buried Bones
11:00 A.M. – 12:15 P.M.	Obstacle Course
12:15 P.M. – 1:00 P.M.	Lunch
1:00 P.M. – 1:30 P.M.	Nap Time
1:30 P.M. – 4:30 P.M.	Obedience Training
4:30 P.M. – 6:00 P.M.	Doggie Massage and Grooming
6:00 P.M. – 7:00 P.M.	Dinner
7:00 P.M. – 9:00 P.M.	Tail-Waggin' Line Dance
9:00 P.M. – 9:15 P.M.	Camp Picture
9:15 P.M. – 10:00 P.M.	Moonlight Stroll
10:00 P.M.	Bedtime

Dog Days of Summer

Use the dog camp schedule to answer the questions.

1. After a big morning of hiking, swimming, and other exercise, the dogs are looking forward to nap time. What fraction of their afternoon (12:00 to 6:00) is spent napping?

2. Jasper was so relaxed after his doggie massage that he was a half hour late for dinner. What time did he finally arrive?

3. Sundae loves to sleep late. If it takes her 10 minutes to eat breakfast, what is the latest time she can show up for breakfast and still be served?

4. New dog owners make sure their puppies go to obedience training. The trainer can see each dog for 30 minutes during the scheduled time. How many dogs can the trainer see?

5. Dexter participated in all of the camp's activities. Not including sleeping and eating, how many hours did Dexter spend at camp?
   a. 10 hours
   b. 12 hours
   c. 9 hours, 2 minutes
   d. 11 hours, 45 minutes

6. Cocoa arrived at camp while the other dogs were finishing lunch. What fraction of the daily activities did she miss?

7. Buddy and Bella went swimming together. They did not see each other again until lunch. How long was it between the times they saw each other?

8. Dudley was tired after an entire day at camp. How many hours long is a day of camp activities?
   a. 12   c. 18
   b. 16   d. 24

9. The chef cooked all of the meals for camp. How much time did she have to prepare lunch after breakfast was over?

10. Howie was the fifth dog in line to complete the obstacle course. If it took each dog an average of 6 minutes to complete the course, what time did Howie finish?

Dog Days of Summer

Use the dog camp schedule to answer the questions.

1. Jake loves the obstacle course. If his owners send him to camp for 4 days while they are on vacation, how much time can he spend on the obstacle course?

2. Buddy left the dance when it was half over, but he stayed for the entire dance the next night. How much time did he spend dancing?

3. There were 20 dogs in the Bone Voyage camp picture. Some dogs were too excited and would not sit still for the picture, so the photographer ran 30 minutes over schedule. If the delay changed the rest of the day's schedule, what time did the moonlight stroll finally begin?

4. Millie ate breakfast as soon as it started. How long was it before she was able to eat again?

5. Winston is a new puppy and needs obedience training. Usually the trainer can see 6 dogs during the scheduled time, but Winston took half of the entire scheduled time. How many dogs, including Winston, could the trainer see?

6. Comeer is a very fast eater. If she eats each meal in 5 minutes, how much free time will she add to her day?

7. Happy's parents were nervous about leaving him alone at camp. They stayed with him until lunch began. If Happy stayed until bedtime, how long did he stay without his owners?

8. Randy was good at finding buried bones. If he found an average of 2 bones every 5 minutes. How many bones did Randy find by the time the next activity started?
   a. 6   c. 30
   b. 12   d. 60

9. Rudy usually sleeps at least 6 hours a day while his owners are at work between 8:00 A.M. and 5:00 P.M. How many fewer hours will Rudy sleep while he is at camp?

10. The price for camp is $2.00 per hour. How much will Sasha's owners pay if Sasha arrives in time for the nature hike and leaves after the camp picture?

Dog Days of Summer

The Picture:

The picture is a schedule for the Bone Voyage Canine Camp. The schedule has a list of activities and the times for the activities.

Teacher Notes:

Schedules can be used for various reasons. Explain to students that some schedules stay the same over time while others may change. Jobs, sporting events, airplanes, and doctors depend on schedules. Schedules keep things running on time so that people can plan how to use the time in each day, week, month, or year. When teaching students a schedule that includes time in a day, it is best to use a clock with hands that advance the hour as the minute hand advances. Introduce the term *elapsed time* to teach students about time that has gone by. Explain that elapsed time can be determined by counting the minutes or hours from a starting time to an ending time. If there are minutes and hours to calculate, students should count the number of minutes from the starting point to the next hour, then count the remaining number of hours. If there are more minutes after the hour, students should calculate them separately. Have students add the minutes and hours together to get total time. For example, to calculate elapsed time from 4:32–6:17, first find the number of minutes from 4:32–5:00 (28 minutes). Then, count the hours from 5:00–6:00 (1 hour). Finally, find the remaining minutes from 6:00–6:17 (17 minutes). The total elapsed time is 1 hour and 45 minutes.

Extension Activities:

1. Have students practice elapsed time using manipulative clocks with hour hands that advance as the minute hands advance. Give students specific activities that happen within the school day, such as lunch or recess. Have them count how many times the minute hand crosses over the 12 to count the hours that will elapse. Begin with times that start and end on the hour, then progress to times that include the half hour.

2. Have students keep track of their daily schedules. Have them write the things they do on a specific day. They should include starting and ending times on their schedules. Ask if they can determine how much time they spend on each activity. To extend this activity, have students keep track of their schedules for a week. Have them compare how the schedules change each day.

3. Speed things up! Keep track of how long it takes for students to do simple things in the classroom, such as line up for lunch, unpack their book bags, or line up for recess. Using a clock with a second hand or a stopwatch, see how long it takes students to do each activity and see if they can improve the time each day. At the end of the week, talk to students about what made things go faster or what obstacles made them go slower.

4. Collect flyers from summer camps in your area. Using a Venn diagram, have students compare and contrast the activities, such as meals, that are similar to those on the dog camp schedule.

Invoice # 21469

VEHICLE DESCRIPTION

SLUGGO'S Deals on Wheels

LAROSA

2005 GX WAGON
7-PASSENGER
2.5 V6 SYSTEM
AUTO TRANSMISSION

EXTERIOR   RED/BLACK TRIM
INTERIOR   TAN/ FABRIC

STANDARD EQUIPMENT INCLUDED:

- AIR CONDITIONING
- AM/FM STEREO CASSETTE
- POWER WINDOWS
- POWER LOCKS
- POWER STEERING
- BUCKET SEATS
- CRUISE CONTROL
- DRIVER AND PASSENGER AIR BAGS
- SEAT-MOUNTED SEAT BELT

PRICE INFORMATION

Manufacturer's
Suggested Retail Price

STANDARD VEHICLE PRICE $18,450

OPTIONAL EQUIPMENT:

PREMIUM AM/FM STEREO/CD PLAYER	$200.00
REAR SEAT DVD ENTERTAINMENT PACKAGE	$1,426.00
SIDE CURTAIN AIR BAGS	$555.00
HEATED FRONT SEATS	$363.00
GPS NAVIGATION SYSTEM	$1,650.00
TOWING PREP PACKAGE	$128.00
POWER SUNROOF	$780.00
FABRIC GUARD	$99.00
LEATHER INTERIOR UPGRADE	$1,560.00
5-PIECE FLOOR MAT SET	$125.00
WINDOW TINT	$70.00
CUSTOM TAPE STRIPE	$60.00
CUSTOM TIRE RIMS	$900.00

VIN: 9 SMI3571113171923 31NC

Fuel Economy Information

CITY MPG

21

HIGHWAY MPG

29

Actual mileage will vary with driving
conditions. The majority of
vehicles will achieve between:
17 and 25 mpg in the city
23 and 34 mpg on the highway

Estimated Annual Fuel Cost:
$792.00

Buying a Car

Use the car invoice to answer the questions.

1. Ben's annual fuel cost is $843.00. If he buys the Larosa, how much money will he save each year?

2. Dale is evaluating how expensive it is to add optional equipment to the car. He is considering adding the floor mat set or the most expensive option on the list. What is the difference between the 2 prices?

3. The Gonzalez family wants to make their Larosa family-friendly. How much will they pay for extras if they add leather interior, rear seat DVD, stereo, and side curtain air bags?

4. Mr. Sluggo, the car dealer, is giving the Gonzalez family a power sunroof and mat set for free. How much would these extras have cost the Gonzalez family?

5. Phil and Frankie buy a Larosa for only $462.00 more than the original price. Which 2 optional features did they add?

6. What is the difference in the number of optional features and standard features the Larosa has?

7. Gary has been saving $100.00 a week for over 3 years to buy a new car. How many $100 bills will Gary need to buy a Larosa?

8. Allison hopes to own her new car for 5 years before she will sell it. How much can she expect to pay in fuel costs for 5 years?

9. Barbara needs a car that does not cost much money to operate. What is the average fuel cost per week for the Larosa?

10. Maya traveled to the beach in her Larosa. Her trip was 145 miles on the highway and 42 miles in the city. If she got the average gas mileage listed on the invoice, how many gallons of gas did she use?

Name _____

Buying a Car

Use the car invoice to answer the questions.

1. Preston wants to customize his car. How much will the final cost be if he adds window tint and a stereo/CD player?

2. Lisa and her husband paid $19,005.00 for the Larosa. What optional safety feature did they buy?

3. If you can drive 435 miles on the highway on a full tank, how many gallons does the fuel tank hold?

4. Patrick needs a car to drive to and from work 20 miles each way through the city. About how many gallons will Patrick use during a 5-day work week?
   a. 9.52   c. 10.11
   b. 9.98   d. 11.34

5. How do you write the ratio of average city miles per gallon (mpg) to average highway miles per gallon?

6. Drew wants a DVD player for his new car. If this is the only optional equipment he adds, about what percentage of the total price of the car is the rear seat DVD package?

7. Thompson wanted a convertible top but settled for another optional feature. If he paid $19,230.00 for the Larosa, what optional feature did he buy?

8. Fuel economy is important when considering a car purchase. What is the average daily fuel cost for the Larosa?

9. If Hal pays 20% down in cash for a Larosa with no added features, how much more will he owe for the car?

10. Stuart is a car salesman. In July, he sold a Larosa for 5% less than the manufacturer's suggested retail price. How much did the customer pay for the car?

Buying a Car

The Picture:
The picture is a sales sticker on the window of a new car. The sticker includes the name, price, options available, and the average fuel economy. Individual options that can be added to the car are also listed with prices.

Teacher Notes:
Students can determine the monthly payments of a car by dividing the price by the number of months of the loan.

Students can determine the number of miles per gallon the car will get by dividing the number of miles given by the city or highway estimates. When given the price per gallon, students can calculate the cost of a trip.

Students can add the prices of additional options to the standard vehicle price to determine the price of the car with options.

Extension Activities:
1. Gather information about different cars and place pictures of them on a bulletin board. Below each picture, place the sticker price for the car. Have students figure the average monthly payment for a five-year loan for each car.
2. Have students keep track of their families' gas mileage for two weeks and compile the data in a class graph. Discuss which car gets the most miles per gallon. Discuss reasons why some cars get better gas mileage than other cars (smaller car, not as heavy as other cars, more highway driving, hybrid vehicle, etc.).
3. Let students plan virtual trips to different destinations in their state. Have them figure the trips' fuel costs using current gas prices in your area.
4. Have students research the difference between hybrid cars, electric cars, and fossil-fuel-only cars and discuss the benefits and drawbacks of each. Let them record the information on a Venn diagram.
5. Help students research safety guidelines for cars. As a class, discuss the importance of cars' safety features and how to use them correctly.
6. Collect data about new cars' prices and what options they include. Have students analyze the prices, options, and fuel economy information and determine which car is the best buy for the money.

Founders' Day Parade Schedule
Information for Parade Officials

Thank you for volunteering to be an official in our annual Founders' Day Parade. Please read all of the instructions below to help make this the best parade ever!

- Please pick up your walkie-talkie, whistle, and clipboard at the 22nd Street Information Center between 9:00 A.M. and 9:45 A.M.
- The parade will begin at exactly 10:00 A.M.
- All marching participants should line up at the starting point 15 minutes before the parade begins.
- The parade will cover 12 blocks. It will travel south on Main Street, beginning at 22nd Street and ending at 10th Street.
- One official should be on the southwest corner of each intersection.
- Officials should arrive at their assigned intersections 10 minutes before the parade begins.
- Participants should travel between intersections at a rate of three minutes per block. Therefore, participants will leave the starting point in three-minute intervals.
- Paramedics will be stationed every five blocks, with the first station located on 22nd Street.
- Officials should blow their whistles one minute before the fire truck is scheduled to arrive at their intersections to clear pedestrian traffic.

Order of Parade Participants:

1. Fire Truck
2. The Mayor in a Convertible
3. Dancing Daisies Dance Team
4. Deering Middle School Marching Band
5. Clowns on Bicycles
6. Founders' Families Float
7. Deering High School Cheerleaders
8. Deering High School Marching Band
9. Adoptable Rescue Animals
10. Founders' Day Princesses in Antique Cars
11. Founders' Day King and Queen Float
12. Police Officers on Horses

A picnic for all parade officials will be held on the elementary school playground 30 minutes after the parade ends. Thank you for all of your help!

I Love a Parade

Use the parade schedule to answer the questions.

1. The Dancing Daisies Dance Team is running 10 minutes late for the parade because of a dance recital at an elementary school. What time will they be at the starting point?

2. Every year, the officials gather before the parade for coffee and doughnuts at a local café. What time do they need to be at their assigned sections this year?

3. The clowns on bicycles like to rehearse before every performance. They rehearse in line before making their entrance. The clowns need to watch the time so that they do not miss their entrance. About what time will the clowns leave the starting point?

4. Kyla is making a list for the officials that includes the time that each parade participant is scheduled to leave the starting point. Which participant will leave the starting point at 10:27 A.M.?

5. Jimmy becomes dehydrated at the parade and needs medical attention. At what block closest to the end of the parade route can his family find paramedics?

6. The City Safety Commission requires a certain number of paramedics per square mile to be at every major parade. How many paramedic stations will there be at this parade?

7. Tawanna came to the parade to see her dad ride with the other police officers on horses. About what time will the police officers leave the starting point?

8. Ms. Arrington is a parade official. She is planning to attend the picnic for the officials after the parade. If the parade ends at 11:09 A.M., what time should she go to the picnic?

9. The Foxes are one of the Founders' Day Families. Based on the 3-minute interval pattern, what time will they leave the starting point?

10. The planning committee needs to buy food and drinks for the picnic. If they buy 1 hot dog, 1 hamburger, and 2 sodas for each official, how many hot dogs, hamburgers, and sodas should they purchase for the picnic?

Name _____

I Love a Parade

Use the parade schedule to answer the questions.

1. The parade committee wants to make an advertisement for the Founders' Day Parade. They want to include the number of blocks that the parade covers. How many blocks is the parade route if each numbered street is between 2 blocks?

2. Javier has football practice after the parade. He needs to know how long the parade will last and if he should leave early to make it to practice on time. If he watches the parade at the starting point, how long will the parade last?

3. The picnic committee needs to estimate the time that they should have the picnic ready. About what time will the picnic for parade officials start?
   a. 10:40 A.M.   c. 12:00 P.M.
   b. 11:45 A.M.   d. 12:15 P.M.

4. Jennica has to leave the parade by 10:20 A.M. If she is standing at the starting point, who are the last participants she will get to see?

5. When should the parade official at 15th Street blow his whistle for the arrival of the fire truck?

6. Jack wants to see the Adoptable Rescue Animals. If he arrives in time to see the Mayor, how long does he have to wait?

7. Maria's little brother Ricky is excited about seeing the fire truck in the parade. He is on 13th street. When will he see the fire truck pass?

8. Mayor Zamora likes to wait until the last minute to make an appearance. At what time should the mayor be ready to start?

9. Amelia's grandfather dropped her off to watch the parade at 14th Street. She was 15 minutes early for the parade to pass this street. What time did she arrive?

10. The newspaper wants a photo of the parade for the Sunday morning edition. If the photographer takes a picture of the participant at 22nd street when the fire truck reaches 15th street, which participant will be photographed?

I Love a Parade

The Picture:
The picture is a parade official's schedule. It includes all of the information an official needs to complete his duties.

Teacher Notes:
The parade begins at 10:00 A.M. If there are 12 parade participants leaving in three-minute intervals, the first participant will leave at 10:00 A.M. and the last participant will start the parade at 10:33 A.M. Encourage students to make lists of participants and when they leave to answer some of the questions.

Explain that the cross streets on the parade route are consecutively numbered and that they cross Main Street in one block intervals.

Extension Activities:
1. Let students organize a parade of books at your school. Have students make posters to advertise the event. Posters should explain that each parade participant can dress as a favorite character or make a banner that includes scenes from a favorite book. Have students determine the length of the parade by determining the number of participants in the parade and the parade route through the school.
2. Discuss why timing of a parade is important. What might happen if the parade participants went too fast or too slow?
3. Discuss parades that students have participated in and what was memorable about them. Then, relate parades to science by talking about the helium needed for parade balloons, how weather affects parade schedules, simple machines used to move parts on floats, etc. Have students look at a community calendar to see what parades will occur in their area in the coming year. Encourage students to attend a parade and notice the science you discussed in action.
4. As a community service project, have students volunteer to help with a parade. (Make sure to get permission from families and the school before allowing students to participate.)

Answer Key

Mixing Music
Page 6
1. "Sum Thing to Add About"
2. 10 songs
3. 32 minutes
4. c.
5. 4:26 P.M. o
6. 27:25
7. *Array of Hope*
8. "Total Ellipse, Not the Heart"
9. *Array of Hope*
10. b.

Page 7
1. *Array of Hope*–32:01
2. *Get to the Vertex*–27:25
3. *Think Outside the Cube*–26:33
4. "Just a Segment"
5. about 45 minutes
6. 2:11
7. "Gee, I'm a Tree"
8. c.
9. yes
10. *Array of Hope*
11. 75%
12. "Let's Be Rational"
13. c.

Checks and Balances
Page 10
1. 10
2. $2,612.30
3. d.
4. $560.45

Page 10 (cont.)
5. $73.65
6. c.
7. $2,400.00
8. $962.29
9. $59.36
10. 20
11. $\frac{3}{4}$

Page 11
1. $2,612.30
2. b.
3. car and satellite
4. April 1
5. Town Square Market
6. $\frac{55}{100}$
7. $537.29
8. 75%
9. $1,476.94
10. no
11. $1,436.76
12. $1,175.58

Calendar Challenge
Page 14
1. 14
2. 11 days
3. February 16
4. 14
5. d.
6. 21 days
7. February 21
8. February 24
9. c.
10. 26 cards
11. 8
12. 20 books

Page 15
1. February 3
2. 5 days
3. b.
4. $60.00
5. 6:15 A.M.
6. 12
7. d.
8. 9 points
9. February 9
10. cat

Grocery Shopping
Page 18
1. $3.78
2. a.
3. Peppy Powder
4. $3.00
5. $5.47
6. b.
7. 5 weeks
8. 1
9. $2.01
10. 6 cups

Page 19
1. $35.69
2. 4
3. $2.75
4. $42.67
5. $31.20
6. a.
7. 27¢ per bagel
8. 20¢ per ounce
9. d.
10. $2.69
11. 3
12. $14.31

Answer Key

Eat at Earl's Diner
Page 22
1. $2.25
2. $42.00
3. c.
4. 12
5. 25¢
6. $3.00
7. d.
8. $4.25; 75¢
9. $\frac{3}{8}$
10. $5.50
11. $\frac{1}{5}$

Page 23
1. $\frac{5}{9}$
2. b.
3. $4.75
4. b.
5. cheeseburger
6. $64.75
7. $12.00
8. 5¢
9. 8
10. 8 Tuesdays

Planning a Garden
Page 26
1. 600 square units
2. 121.5 square units
3. 14 square units
4. c.
5. 1,200 square units
6. d.
7. 16 square units
8. 52 square units
9. 100 square meters
10. 2

Page 27
1. c.
2. b.
3. 140 meters
4. b.
5. rotation
6. 50
7. 4
8. 4
9. $579.00
10. 180

Top of the Charts
Page 30
1. 2.
2. Extraneous
3. 12 weeks
4. 4
5. b.
6. $\frac{9}{10}$
7. 63
8. b.
9. 2
10. 17 weeks
11. d.

Page 31
1. 4
2. The Reflections
3. 11.4
4. 4
5. b.
6. a.
7. $\frac{2}{10}$ or $\frac{1}{5}$
8. Powers of Subtraction
9. Polly Hedron

Let's Go to the Movies
Page 34
1. Sharps Cinema 4
2. $11.00
3. $\frac{3}{4}$
4. Ridgeville Theater 3
5. $42.50
6. 4
7. 13
8. 14
9. 7:30 P.M.
10. 4 tickets at Ridgeville Theater 3
11. c.
12. $23.00

Page 35
1. 4
2. *Circus Ring*
3. The 8:00 P.M showing of *A Dog, a Cat, and a Donkey*, $8.00
4. c.
5. $40.00
6. $8.50
7. 11
8. c.
9. 4:05 P.M at Ridgeville Theater

Weather Watch
Page 38
1. 13 hours and 31 minutes
2. 15°F
3. 38°F; Phoenix (104°F) and San Francisco (66°F)

Answer Key

Page 38 (cont.)
4. San Francisco (66°F)
5. Phoenix
6. Boston
7. Los Angeles
8. 29°F
9. 21°C
10. Wednesday, 20°F

Page 39
1. 15°C
2. 16 hours and 1 minute
3. 89°F
4. c.
5. Salt Lake City, 27°F
6. 92%
7. c.
8. 90.6°F
9. 69°F
10. 36%

Cooking for a Crowd
Page 42
1. 3 cups
2. 6 cups
3. 570 grams
4. d.
5. $7\frac{1}{2}$ cups
6. $16\frac{1}{2}$ cups
7. 3 inches
8. c.
9. 12 cups

Page 43
1. 36 cups
2. string beans

Page 43 (cont.)
3. b.
4. 10%
5. $2\frac{1}{2}$ cups
6. 27 bars
7. $\frac{1}{6}$ cup larger
8. d.
9. 4 batches
10. 18 servings

High Adventures Theme Park
Page 46
1. King's Court
2. 15 ticket book
3. 15 rides
4. $3.00
5. 50¢
6. 45 tickets
7. Jolene
8. $103.55
9. 9 rides
10. c.

Page 47
1. King's Court
2. $351.20
3. 3 tickets
4. $110.00
5. b.
6. 2 adults and either 1 child or one senior
7. $15.00
8. a daily pass
9. $639.80
10. d.

Dog Days of Summer
Page 50
1. $\frac{1}{12}$
2. 6:30 P.M.
3. 7:50 A.M.
4. 6 dogs
5. d.
6. $\frac{3}{7}$
7. 1 hour 45 minutes
8. b.
9. 4 hours 15 minutes
10. 11:36 A.M.

Page 51
1. 5 hours
2. 3 hours
3. 9:45 P.M.
4. 6 hours 15 minutes
5. 4 dogs
6. 3 hours 30 minutes
7. 9 hours 45 minutes
8. b.
9. 5 hours 30 minutes
10. $26.50

Buying a Car
Page 54
1. $51.00
2. $1,525.00
3. $3,741.00
4. $905.00
5. heated front seats and fabric guard
6. 4
7. 185
8. $3,960.00

Answer Key

Page 54 (cont.)
9. $15.23
10. 7 gallons

Page 55
1. $18,720.00
2. side curtain air bags
3. 15 gallons
4. a.
5. 21:29
6. about 7%
7. power sunroof
8. $2.17
9. $14,760.00
10. $17,527.50

I Love a Parade
Page 58
1. 9:55 A.M.
2. 9:50 A.M.
3. 10:12 A.M.
4. Founders' Day Princesses
5. 12th Street
6. 3 stations (22nd, 17th, and 12th)
7. 10:33 A.M.
8. 11:39 A.M.
9. 10:15 A.M.
10. 13 hot dogs, 13 hamburgers, and 26 sodas

Page 59
1. 12 blocks
2. 33 minutes
3. b.

Page 59 (cont.)
4. High School Cheerleaders
5. 10:20 A.M.
6. 21 minutes
7. 16th Street
8. 10:27 A.M.
9. 10:09 A.M.
10. High School Band